Vital Signs

A Play

by Jane Martin

D1468621

A SAMUEL FRENCH ACTING EDITION

SAMUEL FRENCH

FOUNDED 1830

New York Hollywood London Toronto

SAMUELFRENCH.COM

ISBN   978-0-573-62567-1   Printed   in   U.S.A.   #24019

IMPORTANT BILLING AND CREDIT REQUIREMENTS

All producers of VITAL SIGNS *must* give credit to the Author of the Play in all programs distributed in connection with performances of the Play and in all instances in which the title of the Play appears for purposes of advertising, publicizing or otherwise exploiting the Play and/or a production. The name of the Author *must* also appear on a separate line, on which no other name appears, immediately following the title, and *must* appear in size of type not less than fifty percent the size of the title type.

All producers must also show the following credit in all programs distributed in connection with performances of the Play:

"World premiere at the Actors Theatre of Louisville as part of the 1990 Humana Festival of New American Plays."

Vital Signs received a workshop production at Actors Theatre of Louisville from December 5 to 8, 1989. The cast included: Kymberly Dakin, V Craig Heidenreich, Debra Monk, Adale O'Brien, Paul Rogers, Lori Shearer and Pamela Stewart. The stage manager was Frazier W. Marsh.

Vital Signs received its professional premiere production at Actors Theatre of Louisville in the Humana Festival of New American Plays. It opened March 21, 1990 and played through March 31. The cast included: Kymberly Dakin, Randy Danson, V Craig Heidenreich, Adale O'Brien, Paul Rogers, Priscilla Shanks, Pamela Stewart and Myra Taylor. The stage manager was Frazier W. Marsh, the scenic designer was Paul Owen, the lighting designer was Victor En Yu Tan, the sound designer was Mark Hendren, props master was Mark Bissonnette, and the costume designer and dramaturg was Marcia Dixcy.

Many thanks to Richard Trigg for use of his premiere production photograph in this acting edition.

ACT ONE

ACT TWO

Appendix

SETTING: The stage is empty except for three chairs. One is overstuffed, massive, providing sitting areas on the arms and back with a matching hassock in front of it. One is a rocking chair. One is a vinyl fifties kitchen chair. The surround is black.

Director's Note

Vital Signs is performed by six women and two men. Though the play is a series of monologues, there is constant interaction between its cast members. Some pieces are played directly to audience members using them as characters. Some are played to other actors. Some are performed as internal monologues. In some pieces, such as "Nintendo Woman" and "Cocaine Hotline", non-speaking actors create the world of a video game arcade or office with mimed characters. Occasionally a piece has the element of a duologue with exchanged lines. Often other actors are onstage listening to another actor work. The more a director uses these means to provide variety and a sense of ensemble, the more powerful and funny the evening becomes.

The play uses only three chairs with no other scenery. The only prop is a tray of hor d'oeuvres. The costumes should be the actors' own rehearsal clothes. Lights shift to provide atmosphere, but there are no blackouts until the end of the act and the end of the evening.

Recorded music is useful behind certain pieces, such as "Encyclopedia Salesmen," "Truck Stop," "One Moment," and "Endings," but should not be overused. Flow is everything. The pieces should follow each other quickly, preventing, when possible, internal applause.

Characterization is important but should not give the impression of broad strokes or heavy use of dialect. The director will find that what gives this work its special flavor is the quick internal movement from comedy to something more painful, or vice versa, in a single two-minute piece.

The order has been determined to provide variety, help the pieces inform each other, and provide a movement toward a somewhat darker coloration by evening's end.

An appendix of four other pieces is provided as possible substitutions if cast composition would make them useful.

BEGINNINGS

A WOMAN sits on the back of the overstuffed chair with her feet on the seat. Also onstage are the CHARACTERS for the two pieces to follow. THEY listen.

So, uh, invariably I'm uh, well, better at the uh ... well I'm better at the start, at the beginning ... or so I'm, well, generally told that uh, that I am ... at the beginning ... of ... of ... well I guess almost anything. Affairs ... jobs, absolutely on jobs ... trips, always better the first hour on trips ... hors d'oeuvres, never want anything after the hors d'oeuvres ... it's uh ... well, I guess it's a, you know, a pattern ... they usually tell me. So. See at the beginning I never, ever seem to know what I'm ... It all seems very ... full of possibilities ... very romantic ... very ... and then when I'm still thinking that I find out I'm in the middle ... well for me the middle is ... well I experience flight syndrome ... middle panic ... middle muddle ... and uh, characteristically the middle seems pointless ... and of course no one likes being around someone feeling pointless so actually it's the end. But ah ... strangely enough ... well the end ... I don't mind the end because uh ... well the end is that much closer to the beginning ... so uh ... so I'm terrifically relieved

... really ... because I know I'll shine in the beginning, which makes me more fun at the end. Sort of. So honestly ... to be fair ... I ... well. I try to, you know, warn people that the beginning is in a way, well, the end. But it doesn't help because well, and this, this is the uh bad part, I'm usually attracted to linear thinkers who like to uh, move forward, so we never stay in the beginning so it uh ... it uh ... doesn't work out.

SUPREME LIGHT

*A WOMAN kneels beside a MAN sleeping on his
back on the floor.*

WOMAN. Hi, I've got sort of a moral
dilemma, can I counsel with you? Our supreme
light and pillar of universal enlightenment, he of
the thousand eyes, Uraja Pradesh Mahavira, may
he radiate forever, who has gathered the disciples
of joy from every state and sixteen nations to
build his temple in Butte, Montana, has received
vibrations from on high that his German
shepherd, Rusty, wishes to lie with me. No,
really. I know this body is but the cup for the
river that is always running and that pleasure is
the gift of the material self for the delectation of
the spirit of others but this kind of pisses me off.
Look, I sold my Nash Rambler and rendered up
the money. I made over the checking account and
accepted the daughter of delighted poverty ring. I
have sung the fifteen simplicities over and over on
six months of latrine gift, and chanted with full
heart while we hauled the four hundred tons of
creek rock to build the Palace of World Peace and
Erotic Meditations but this is where I draw the
line.
MAN. Nine generations ...

WOMAN. Sure, nine generations of supreme ones inhabit each micro-iota of my master's words but I was born in Trenton, New Jersey, and there is one doo-doo I don't step in.

MAN. Laura!

WOMAN. So I guess what I'm saying is this: I'm giving you my parabolic prayer rug and beads of the sixth union. I'm setting fire to my tent and bedroll. I ritually break the mantra thread that ties me to the universe to come and I'm blowing this joint, Larry. What I want is a Coors beer, some French fried onion rings, and the first Methodist church I can find. Rudyard Kipling was right about never-the-twain. Don't take up a religion your mother can't spell.

COCAINE HOTLINE

The entire COMPANY creates an office mime as background for MS. BOTTENDORF:

Good morning, Cocaine Hotline, Ms. Bottendorf here to help you break the cycle of despair. Uh, huh. Uh, huh. Uh, huh. Well, I don't really see anything we can do if you're going to behave like that. (*SHE hangs up.*) Will somebody get me a Diet Pepsi for God's sake before I start screaming and trying to get my tongue into my Panasonic pencil sharpener. What kind of society is this!

(PHONE rings, SHE answers it.)

Good morning, Cocaine Hotline. Uh, huh. Uh, huh. Uh, huh. Uh, huh. Hold it right there. All right, Cornelia, you called for advice. I am giving you advice. Tell him you are flat out going to leave his ass. Uh, huh. Well, that's just too bad. Tell him when he wants help he can write you a letter. Tough Tootsie Rolls, Cornelia. You have to cut off the sex, cut off the money. Figure out the one thing he wants, Cornelia, and cut that mother off! If you do not act, and I mean before the sun sets, he's going to nosebleed his life all over your prairie-pattern quilts. Yes, well take it or leave it. I have three calls waiting. (*Hangs up. Stands up.*) I would like to say to all of you here at Cocaine Hotline that we are going down, going down with the ship, and we are out of Diet Pepsi, folks. No society can help itself without a constant supply of diet drinks that you can count on. I'm taking a john break. Let me know if the country buys the farm.

30 HOURS

One actress sits on the hassock and speaks to other ACTORS on the stage.

Everybody has about 30 hours of conversation, after that it's all reruns. Ordinarily, a person can do about twelve hours on their family, ten on their past, five on their divorce, three on their present and maybe forty-five minutes of personal philosophy. My theory is that almost anyone can be interesting for three dates which means you've usually been to bed with him before you discover he's a tape. The best I ever met rang in at 200 hours but it was all on Suzuki motorcycles which kept putting me to sleep. "Cranks were trued to blah, blah, blah ... intake adapters blah, blah ... carbs on the Honda/Webco 350 blah, blah, blah." It made me pray for an awkward silence. Every ten years we ought to be heard by a Board of Examiners who should tattoo a conversational rating to our foreheads. That way you could *get out* before it *ran out.* Ever try ten years of marriage on six hours of conversation? If it weren't for gossip, children or grocery shopping, ninety percent of all marriages would be conducted in silence. The only ones without a limit are deeply neurotic, desperately narcissistic, drop-dead alcoholic or have dangerous criminal minds. All in all, it's a bleak picture. (*Pause.*) Say something.

LOTTO

This ACTRESS enters from offstage and plays the piece with an AUDIENCE MEMBER.

I got the Lotto. I got it. I got all six numbers. Shhhh. I haven't showed this to nobody. Shhh. Here ... you hold the ticket ... help me check it out. Shoot, I looked a hundred times but Lord, I don't trust myself. (*Calls out the numbers.*) Six, three, one. They say it's $5.5 million in twenty-one installments. Lord in Heaven! I work down to the Hercules Cleaning Service. Well, it's a very rewarding thing to remove filth. People like you to do it. My husband, Joe, he's a retired insurance adjustor, and he does part-time lawn mower repair. We have a 1947 DeSoto. Original upholstery. That's our pride an' joy. They say that woman won ten million last year picked her up a bad nervous condition. She's in a peck of tax trouble and divorced her a husband she had thirty years. Joe and me we worked all these years to get our lives right. We're orderly in that way. I don't think they like you to clean or drive some old DeSoto with money like that. Seven, four, nine. Oh, my. My Momma, rest her soul, she always said, "If it ain't broke, don't fix it," "Don't trade the cow for a milk truck," things like that.

(*Pause.*)

Here, you keep it. You're more young and
better situated for it. Put it in your purse. Shhhh.
Go on. Do what I told you. Go on. And don't tell
Joe. That's the way we are. He leaves the details
to me.

COLD WAR

This piece is played to other ACTORS who find her political stance slightly embarrassing.

Gee, really this ...ummm ... sort of ... well, embarrassing but ... all right, straight out ... I miss the Cold War. I do. I liked ... oh, God ... I liked being afraid of the Russians. At least it made Reagan bearable, you know? Now, they're, gosh, the two of them, like artifacts, you know, like old newsreels, but they're still playing in my theatre. It's like having to tell your President his fly is open. Pssss, George ... get out of the tank, George ... it's tacky to ride around in a tank now, trust me. But with no Russians, boy, who am I going to hate now? Myself probably. Boy, I used to say to myself, Cathy, boy are you behaving like a jerk. You are really screwed up. Boy, Cathy are you ever leading an unexamined life, but ... who cared, you know, because BOOM! Adios! Nuclear winter.

Now I'm going to have to live with myself, you know? Christ, who needs it? Instantaneously, no Lenin, no Marx, no Communism. The first thing they wanted from us, buddy was a McDonald's. A McDonald's. Think about it. You know what that means. It means we're going to be up to our ass in styrofoam cups and pop tops.

One world, right? One big mouth is more like it.
One giant mouth, world tongue, universal craw
snarfing up everything in the refrigerator and
then, then, boy, we'll start in on each other *again,*
only meaner and hungrier and drugged up to our
eyeballs until we're living in a pig wallow, cutting
each other's throats over potato peelings and
calling it an inalienable right.

Hey, remember the graffiti on the Berlin wall?
"We came, we saw, we did a little shopping."
Sure shopping, they should have shopping, but
... I don't know ... maybe I'm empathy dead. I'm
scared. It's stupid. I'm scared, O.K.? Don't look
at me that way, I'm a liberal. O.K., I'm wrong.
Tell me what to think.

TRUCK

All the WOMEN sit or stand around the overstuffed chair. They are the truck stop's cafe employees. A male ACTOR enters and takes their picture with a flash camera.

Me? I waitressed at the only all-nude truck stop in West Virginia. It kinda caught on. We was all jaybird naked, cooks, cashiers, bus girls, the bunch of us. We'd flip to see who worked the tables near the front door in December. Guy pulls a twelve-cyclinder, 456 horsepower Detroit Diesel into the lot. Slides into my booth in a white silk suit with a tie with a diamond stud. Says he's the one, the only, Reverend Billy Frost, got him a sixteen wheel ministry an' the home phone number of the Holy Ghost. "Good evenin' little lady," he says, "I take you to be in the Garden of Eden or tied to the spokes of the wheel of fire. Now I'll have me a decaf Cappucino and a side order of small curd cottage cheese, an' when I leave, senorita, you're invited to ride." Slipped his silk coat over my shoulders, offered me his arm, walked me past the truckers to an all white rig, says "Resurrection Express" in letters of flame. "Climb up, little lady," he says, "leave the dust of the road behind you." His eyes were serene as a hawk on an updraft, so I did.

Sang hymns, shouted scripture, and screwed me seven times on the way to Laramie, Wyoming. Left me by the side of the road at this deep pan pizza parlor run by two Koreans. (*S H E approaches a male actor.*) Disappointed? Well, that's a real luxury in a life like mine, sailor. I got to generally trust any human being ain't armed or got blood on their shoes. Tell you what. Buy me a beer and give me a ride into Palm Springs, you can tell me *your* modus operandi.

ARBY'S

The ACTRESS sits speaking to several other women.

WOMAN. Honey, what the tight asses never teach you in school is when the end is. I'd known that I'd saved me about twelve years in two marriages. My second finally sat me down said, "Marjorie Ann, you been screwin' around on me for seven years, haven't slept with me in six months, haven't talked to me in ten days, now I filed for divorce this afternoon, I figured I better tell you so you'd notice when I'm gone." (*Laughs.*)

I'm a good lookin' woman an' I have me some fun but I just don't have me a sense of conclusion. They say it ain't over 'til it's over? Hell, with me it ain't over 'til well over when it's over, an' sometimes it's not over 'til two overs over that. (*Laughs.*) I spent three days in Acapulco with a fella was an architect for Arby's Roast Beef. (*Pause. Male ACTOR enters.*)

Hell, I thought those things just sprung up over night like mushrooms, didn't you? (*Laughs.*) He said when you have a structure you see when it fulfills itself and it's just naturally over.

MAN. Like a circle.

WOMAN. He said.

23

MAN. You draw a circle you know when it's finished.

WOMAN. Honey, I told him the trouble is you'd damn well know that before you started so what the hell's the fascination? Oh, I put me together some odd shapes in my life, darlin', but they never did look nothin' like an Arby's Roast Beef! I start somethin' and then generally move on when somethin' shiny catches my eye, like a crow does. It's just one lopsided damn thing sittin' next to another lopsided damn thing, how I see it. Don't fit together any way you can make sense of, do they?

Third day with the architect we was waitin' for the elevator and outta nowhere he asked me to marry him! Honey, I was so God-damned surprised I said yes. (*Male ACTOR exits.*) Elevator door opens, he steps in ... Fell fourteen floors down an empty shaft. Now he lived, but the subject of marriage never came up again. (*Laughs.*)

Drawing the circle. Huh-uh, not my style, darlin'. Honey, I'll just scribble some good lookin' shit 'til I run out of paper. I don't want to see the structure 'til they turn out the lights.

BUSINESS WOMAN

The ACTRESS sits in a chair near the audience and plays the piece to an older male patron.

I don't feel there's a significant difference between us on this issue, Mr. Carlyle. I am willing to artificially depress our prices forcing you into a price war because it is my educated guess that our pockets are a little deeper and our markets a little better situated and we don't have the same need for fluidity and capital that a little bird tells me you do. There is, as I'm sure you're aware, a natural process of selection in business as my father used to say, "When it's time to go, it's time to go." Now in my opinion, you've had your innings and in a nice way, a very nice way, you've become a superfluous and even, though I don't like to say this, an inhibiting factor in an expanding market. Your options, Mr. Carlyle, are to sell or fold. It's Florida time, Mr. Carlyle, which can't be too unpleasant a prospect given the time you already spend on the links. Well, I've got a lunch and you've got a lunch so when you've run this by your people give me a call. Oh, one more thing. I greatly appreciate the fact that during all those years we worked together you were punctilious about treating me as an equal and colleague and not simply as your daughter. You can be assured in the changed circumstances that I will do the same for you. Sorry, have to run.

QUALITY TIME

EVERYONE exits except the ACTRESS who plays the piece alone on an imaginary playground.

Anna, Anna, honey, the slides's hot, honey, don't go down the slide without your bathing suit. No, no, no.

Billy, Billy! Get out from behind the swings! Further back, even further. You know what Mommy told you about swings.

Anna, Anna, some people don't like to see us without our bathing suits. Sick as that may be. Come get a towel from Mommy, sweetie.

Greg! Let go of her hair! Yes, I know it's your truck. No, she doesn't like it, Greg, she is screaming.

Little girl? Give him back the truck, darling, he's ruthless. It is his truck. Give him back the ...

Anna, not in the sand pile ... yes I know we do that at home ... Oh, my God, Anna ... cover it up ... put sand over it ... with your foot ... no, don't pick it up! Billy, make Anna put it down ... Billy... not with the plastic bucket, Billy ...

Greg, stop it! She doesn't want to be in the tire. Good. No. She doesn't want to be on the see-saw. No sand fights, Billy. Greg, do not brush her off there. Because her mommy doesn't like it.

Anna, not in the fountain!

Billy, stop picking at it, it's a scab.

Do not hit foreign mommies, Greg. I'm sorry. I'm sorry. I'm sorry.

Billy! (*A pause. SHE watches the carnage.*)

Quality time.

IMPOTENCE

*A WOMAN sits on the overstuffed chair talking to
another ACTRESS sitting on the hassock. In
the middle of the piece a MAN enters and lies
down on the floor. The PERFORMER moves
to the man and lies down as if she were in bed
with him.*

The moving van pulls away. I monitor myself
for a reaction. What? What am I feeling? In point
of fact I'm ecstatic. The marriage is gone, he's
gone, the furniture is gone, I feel great! Then I
make a mistake and look in the mirror. Is anybody
going to find *this* attractive? I get instantaneous
depression. I'm ugly. Not to worry. My first
week I have three dates. All right, two of them
were married, but I'm still counting them as dates.
I'm enthusiastic and sleep with all of them. It
turns out they have one thing in common. They're
all impotent. This is what they don't tell you when
you get a divorce. Melly, what is going on? I
worried available men would be ego-monsters
dripping arrogance and command; they're not,
they are sweet, vulnerable guys who have caught
some kind of sexual flu. They're in agony, they
weep, they rage, you have to take Kleenex to bed.
I decide all men from 10 p.m. to 7 a.m. are living
on an outpatient basis—poor babies! They must

exist in this paroxysm of dread. Completely focused on what they can't control. Totally defined by an irrational muscle. Passionately believing it's all that matters. Found out despite the rest of their lives. One of them told me it was like cradling a corpse between his legs. And my job ... my job is to fix it. Or else to console the inconsolable. And all of this ... all of his pain, all of my responsibility, locked in a horrified panic reaction to the absence of six seconds of abandon. And this, Melly, this is my dream of sexual freedom. Gosh, it makes me long for the security of a bad marriage.

NINTENDO WOMAN

The entire COMPANY supports the SPEAKER by creating an imaginary arcade. This is a very physically active piece.

Blast that sucker, Earth Girl ... wo-wo-wo-wo-wo-boom ... Nintendo woman ... hit it yattata-yattata-yattata smash ... mobile unit, tank crusher fifteen degrees right ... Shawham! Got that bitch-mother, yes! You lookin' at the one, the only, the arcade Goddess of East St. Louis, fella. Eat green slime space station drone! I stayed eight straight hours on Karma-Blaster for one quarter, man. I saved the princess of the moon of Jupiter nine times on Planet Warrior left-handed, seven times right-handed, two times with my teeth, an' once with my genitalia. Missile one, missile two, all side turrets now! Hey, players, Kerrack! Look me over, stick monkeys. Do I reign supreme? Step on up if you're cool to my heat. State your name and pick your game, suckers. This is the *real,* jockeys, an' out there, out the arcade, is the no program, unbeatable, featureless, creatureless slough of despond. Don't go out there, babies! In here it's a quarter a game. But out there it's without price. No control! Whack! You have no control! Slam! We got Rocket-Tank, Black Asteroid, Slime People, Cobra Carrier, Lost

31

Worlds of the Snake Robots. Stay with me. Stay safe, players, It's spoiled out there, on tilt, out of order, computers down. Let it go. Let it be, babies! Quarters all around. Sha-bam! Play it up!

IGUANA

An ACTRESS and ACTOR sit on the floor with their backs against the overstuffed chair and their feet on the hassock as if they were in bed.

I had me a pet iguana. Silver, green. Tied a red bow on him 'cause he moved fast. Kept in the shadows. Bought him at an outdoor art fair. Halloween present. My brother's wife wouldn't have him in the house. I didn't mind. Fed him a regular line of flies. He was voracious. I started datin' this guard dog trainer was a Viet Nam vet. Real nice and reserved. Met him out to the fairgrounds at the Fish and Game show. Had forearms big as my waist. Wore a shoulder holster. Even in bed. We'd put on Grateful Dead tapes, drink pina coladas, fool around all day. Sat bolt upright in the Pullman bed. "Oh, oh," he says, "Incoming," he yells. Pulls a .45. "Infiltrators!" His eyes was all pupil. Nostrils flared. "You ain't cuttin' off my balls." Starts firin'. I flattened back on the head board. Used up the clip. There was holes in the trailer and iguana on every flat surface in the room. "I think you got him," I said. "Fucking Cong," he says. Fell back, slept fourteen hours. I never tried to replace the iguana. There are just certain things you shouldn't own because of the way the world is. Certain

33

things you shouldn't do either, but I'm not gettin'
into that.

I LOVE YOU

An ACTRESS sits on the floor and pulls a MAN down to lie in her lap. The piece ends in a kiss. THEY freeze.

I love you. Always before I've had to love on speculation. I could call it by its name but I knew it had a shelf life. Sort of the top of something that I knew was on the way down. Saying "I love you" was just pointing out your position on a loop. It was how you described a high point. Someone was beautiful and I loved that. Someone cut through the bullshit and I loved that. Someone made me, thank God, forget myself and I loved that. But never, never was I crazy enough to turn myself over to it. As soon as I said it, I made damn sure I had it on a leash and I knew it died from repetition. The bottom line for me were the couples in restaurants who never say a word while they eat. I knew it all was reduced eventually to silence. Until you made it safe for me. No matter what happens, you always pay attention. Imagine that. To most people, paying attention is merely part of the acquisition. You pay attention so I can take myself seriously so I can take you seriously, so I pay attention. It's a miracle. I love you.

FRIED CHICKEN

*The ACTRESS sits in the vinyl chair, or is
already there. SHE speaks dully and without
emotion.*

So he asked where his dinner was and I said it
was almost midnight. He grabbed me by the hair
and said get him food. I said get it himself. He hit
me in the face with the heel of his hand and I
could feel my nose break. He pulled me into the
kitchen and I fought. He turned on the stove and
forced my hand down onto the burner. Get me a
beer he said, so I did. He said food so I put my
hand in a sandwich bag full of ice and started to
fry him some chicken. He told me wash, he didn't
want blood in the eats. I said fuck you under my
breath and he threw the beer. It hit me in the
breast. He put me on the floor and said if it was a
fuck I wanted, well a fuck I'd get. He ripped my
clothes and did it to me from behind. Then he told
me to bring him the chicken. I gave it to him. He
ate and went into the TV room and watched a
game. He fell asleep. I got the grill starter and
poured it over him and lit it. He slapped at himself
like there was mosquitos and then sat up straight
and asked was something burning? Then he ran
right through the glass sliding porch door and
died on the patio. I changed the channel and

watched *Hawaii Five-O* but it was a repeat. Then I called you. My hand hurts. Oh my Jesus.

HOR D'OEUVRES

A genial, cheerful WOMAN in a white server's jacket enters with an hors d'oeuvres tray and passes them out to the audience during her speech.

I been circulating hors d'oeuvres at white people's parties for a good many years. I like 'em. White people I mean. The hors d'oeuvres vary. It's kinda general callin' them "white people." So I'll just call 'em Tiffany and William, all right? Tiffany and William they're a little handicapped but they're still functional. Now I got a limited perspective but they can definitely eat hors d'oeuvres and call you by your first name. Tiffany and William they got problems, but shoot, we all do. Main problem is a sense of humor. They never laugh when they see a whole bunch of white people eating hors d'oeuvres and a bunch of black people servin' 'em. I laugh all the time. Tiffany likes it, she likes to see me happy. William, well I always call him Mr. Barnes, he always says to me, "Good evenin' Lona, how are you doin'?" An' I always say, "Fine and dandy but for my back problems, Mr. Barnes." An' he always says, "Well, Lona, we're not getting any younger." Then he smiles an' takes two bacon-wrapped chicken livers an' claps me on the back.

Tiffany, she always pat me and ask how my little girl is an' I say "Henry doin' fine," an' she pat me some more an' say she got some dresses from her little girl if I want. Tiffany, she always passes on the bacon-wrapped chicken livers.

They sort of pre-occupied too. I go by 'em on the street six, seven times a year but they don't see me. Oh, maybe if I had my hors d'oeuvres.

Yes, I like white people. Umm. Tiffany and William. They so happy runnin' things, an' dressin' nice, an' shootin' game, playin' tennis an' eatin' hors d'oeuvres. Poor things. I think they're a little ... well, you know ... not quite right. Well, we can't fix everything in this old world. I know that. We just got to feed 'em an' be nice to 'em, hope they have the best time they can. They kind of a lesson really. Can't everybody be black. (*SHE exits.*)

TRICK SHOT

An actress alone on stage.

They call me 20-20. I'm a trick shot artist. I can pepper a copper plate three foot by three foot, draw you a portrait of any American president with forty-eight shots. Fifty-four for Roosevelt 'cause of the cigar. I can shoot off the wick on a candle or put six holes in a Dr. Pepper before it strikes the earth. I fell in love with a Lebanese rope dancer called Mademoiselle Sofie at the Louisiana State Fair, and she with me, an' we hit out in tandem. She was a long drink of water with eyes like plums and hair that just touched her ankles. Taught her a few easy shots like the silver dollar throw 'cause there's a moment it don't rise or fall so you're just pluggin' a stationary object, but mainly she was the "holder." Held apricots, long stem roses, and a glass ballerina I shot cupped in the palm of her hand. We done country fairs down through the asshole of the south 'til it got too chill to shoot. In a Motel Six in Tupelo, Mississippi, I caught her in a single bed with an animal trainer just out of jail runnin' a mangy chimp and pekinese basketball act. Next day I blew off her right hand holdin' the ace of spades at a thousand booth flea market. Now I didn't mean to do it, but it was hell to explain in the circumstances. I guess it always gets down to travelin' alone, don't it? Love being the fickle pursuit it is, there ain't a whole lot of people wantin' a short-term romance with anybody's as good a shot as I am. It's a hopeless damn thing tryin' to mix a full-time career with a long-term relationship. You know when her hand hit the ground it held onto the card? Surprised the hell out of me. Funny how the best things you do in this life you couldn't do twice if you tried.

(*The LIGHTS dim to black.*)

ACT II

CHORALE

The entire COMPANY is onstage. As the LIGHTS come up THEY applaud as if at an awards celebration. The ACTRESS holds up her hands for silence. SHE speaks.

I would like to thank my father Augustus (*More applause*.) Lee for running off with the music teacher and leaving a note on the ice box and being heard from subsequently on major holidays and showing up late and leaving early at selected funerals. (*More applause*.)

I would like to thank Uncle Charlie for explaining that men were always hot for it and would tell you anything to get it and to watch out all the time and be alone with them as little as possible. (*More applause*.)

I would like to thank Luke BeJart for finally getting me out of my clothes without saying anything at all and then going off to the University of Maryland and becoming a Trappist monk.

I would like to thank my first husband Jackie for being kind and patient and nurturing and understanding and ultimately gay.

I would like to thank the fourteen men I slept with in 1981 for the yeast infections, non-specific urethritis, the abortion, the week in St. Croix, the terrible blank verse and considerable satisfaction.

I would like to thank Carl the lawyer for my child Jeremy even though it wasn't right for him to get a divorce given his wife's dependency and history of depression, and the fact that she wouldn't give him the house.

I would like to thank my second husband Allen and his teenage children Joyce, Danielle and Tim for doing the best they could until it became obvious that the majority of us didn't like each other and some of us didn't flush the toilet.

I would like to thank Matvey the Czechoslovakian emigre plumber with the haunted eyes and high cheekbones for being interested even if I can't sleep with him right now and for bringing me that hand carved, hand painted box and the wonderful recording of the Male Chorus.

I'm in good shape now. Really. Thanks. Did I leave anyone out?

(LIGHTS cross-fade.
The attention immediately shifts to a WOMAN sitting in the rocker. SHE addresses both the cast and the audience.)

SKINS

Skin players, stick, ooo-ee yes uh-huh. Mamie Le Smile, now, Mamie Le Smile, ooo-eee. She had a bitchin' left hand and speedo speed, she did. She could sling a riff so sweet, wouldn't nobody jam, for fear they weren't up to it. The best lady drummer, no kiddin', that's flat. She was, she was, oh yes. Had six, she did, six brothers yes. They was two sax, two bass, one mortician and a real bad mental went down in an armed robbery at the Cut-Rate, corner of Marshall and Lagoon. Kansas City was her town and renown. She sit in at the One Note, flog them men drummers clean outta the room. Catch-you-later, so long, piss off! You wanted some weed, some seed, a sawbuck, or some late night blues, oh she was the one, she was. Did the road for two years with Basie, but she was a car sick so she cashed it in. Had her picture in *Life* magazine, half sweat an' half smile, dicen' them sticks so quick they was gone from the photo. Whoosh! Hell, she could make a blur look like a back beat, yes. Sure, she playin' weekends when she was eighty years old an' stone bone blind did Mamie Le Smile. Eighty-third birthday led the whole bar outside singin' "Cajun Lady," yells "fuck it," steps out in front of the 10th Street bus. Bam! Sure she died but she was survived by a thirty-six

47

hundred dollar dent set a record on that particular model. Word got out it started leakin' drummers, rainin' drummers, deluged with drummers, oh yes. Scootch Gissel took him a cab from Chicago, driver tossed him the keys, say "You bought it my man, you in the taxi business." Stick men by thumb, stick men by limos, bikin', hikin', pullin' their sets in red Flyer wagons. They was triplin' the price on hotel rooms. Funeral day, yes took an hour seventeen minutes for those headlights to pass her bar. After that they laid out three hundred sets in the Pick Pac parkin' lot, played them a 30 minute riff off "After You've Gone" you could hear in L.A. stood up an yelled "Fuck It" and drank themselves away by the light of the moon. Mamie Le Smile. Hell, I bet she'd screwed two thirds of 'em. She had a bitchin' left hand an' she always left a drink in the bottle. God bless her tart ass. Bottoms up. (*SHE mimes downing a drink.*)

ENCYCLOPEDIA SALESMAN

With the FULL CAST still onstage listening, the ACTRESS addresses the audience.

Oh, I love those boys who sell encyclopedias with their bright eyes and souls! Always dressed so nice, every bit as good as the Mormon missionaries, if you ask me. You will never see a grease spot on their ties, it is completely unheard of and that's a fact. Oh, they come to do the mind honor and they dress to fit. I'm on all the lists: Encyclopedia Britannica, World Book, Compton's, House of Knowledge, Facts Illustrated, all of them. I always try to fix them a nice little something, maybe a quiche and some vegetable juice, nothing heavy. Then I sit right down in the hallway, with my heart pounding so I can catch the doorbell on the first ring.

There is such a lovely formality to it all that it reminds me of the days when there was such a thing as society. And the graces. I pull back the wing chairs in the living room so he can spread out his full color charts and graphs and maps and samples and I curl up on the sofa with my tea and the conversation just buoys us up and carries us along as if we were sitting with our harps in the clouds. We usually start out with the Brazilian Rain forest and work our way right through stars and stellar populations to Yiddish literature and the Haskala traditions and sometimes dark will fall without our noticing and the ideas they will actually perfume the air. Oh, if there's a life of the mind now, it's in encyclopedia sales. And those boys, those dear boys, it's quite usual after you've given them the check for them to kiss your hand when they leave, and smile and smile until your heart nearly breaks.

JAY

This piece begins with the ACTRESS sitting but early on SHE rises, moves the hassock stage right of the armchair with her foot and ends sitting on it.

See, my vocation is giving pleasure. People are mainly scared of people. I read where most people only have two or three friends in a whole life, plus a couple of marriages. I was the high school mascot for the North Broderick Bears an' I saw right off I was more popular as a bear than a person. There was always somebody wantin' to pet me, play with me, tryin' to look up my nose hole, see who I really was. Right then I knew I was meant for it. Went on to be the Virginia Tech Hokie, sort of a turkey kind of thing, which was good as it gave me bird experience. Later on I kind of free-lanced as a fresh water shrimp, and a year down at Disneyland as Daisy Duck, but that was generally too heavy a drug scene. My big break came at the National Baseball Card Show in Miami, where I did day work as the Toronto Blue Jay. Well, I wasn't on the floor an hour before I got real attracted to the St. Louis Cardinal. Talk about your chemistry! We started rubbin' up to each other, whew, got so hot we snuck off to the broom closet. Guy heard something going on,

opened the door, saw two giant birds in among
the cleaning fluids screwin' like they was an
endangered species. Well, there were these little
flaps. That guy laughed so hard he started to
choke an' I had to do the Humperdink maneuver
on him to save his life. Turned out he was
marketing manager for the Jays, so he got me on
to work the fans. I'm not out in public as a human
more than eight, ten hours a month. Humans
these days don't have a sense of mystery. They're
pretty much what they are which is why they love
me. Shoot, I wouldn't ever come out I didn't have
to. Oh, I'm into it. I go sky diving for the full
effect. It's a real shame it's come down to where
you have to leave your own species for a good
life. That's just about the end of the road I guess.

(*The full CAST exits except for the ACTRESS
doing "Graceland" who puts on a pair of
glasses and moves up behind the armchair.*)

GRACELAND

A young WOMAN on and off mike at the Graceland Reception Center.

Good morning and welcome to Graceland, a division of Elvis Presley Enterprises. If you are buying tickets for the homes, grounds, or attractions ... is this thing on? Hello? ... homes, grounds, or attractions, please follow the blue line between the blue ropes. What's that? I'm in the middle of an announcement, sir ... are you looking for the Elvis recreational bus or the automobile museum? Combo ticket one for all attractions is available for $15.95. That includes ... sir, you in the "I got bombed at the Strategic Air Command Visitors Center" tractor hat, we would prefer you did that in your bedroom with a woman, ostensibly your wife. Sir, Combo 2 includes the automobile museum but not the bus. No, sir, there is no combo that includes the Lisa Marie jet airplane but not the auto museum. Because I say so. I am not at liberty to say why. Because that is what Elvis wants you to see on Combo 2. I do not appreciate being called four-eyes, sir, when all I have is astigmatism. Get outta my face, sucker. Sir, I cannot let you in, in any case, wearing a Mick Jagger Altamont jacket. Because, sir, Elvis Presley died for your sins, and

Mick Jagger is the Anti-Christ. Mick Jagger never recorded a Christmas song in his life, or served in the Army, or knew his gospel. He represents the foreign, bi-sexual annihilation of the rock-and-roll dream and he don't set a foot in this sanctuary with you or without you! Next! (*SHE exits.*)

FATHER'S CIRCLE

The ACTRESS enters talking and sits in the rocker. SHE is alone onstage.

My father wasn't in my life exactly. If you drew a circle around a life he would be sitting just outside with his feet on the line, reading a book. Once, out of nowhere, like coming into focus ... I was twelve, I think ... he stood up from the chair and took me on the ferry to Coney Island. It was like a date. I wore my black and white skirt with the rust blouse and two bows in my hair. I never wore bows but I wanted to look like a daughter. We went to the aquarium and saw Ookie, the gentleman walrus. It was a triumph. The keeper asked me to pet him. "Give him a kiss," he said, "Ookie likes the ladies." He had a papery feeling against my lips. My father laughed and clapped his hands. Actually clapped his hands. And then he took my arm and I remember looking at passersby to see if they knew we were a father and daughter. On the ferry ride back, we sat side by side and sang "Daisy, Daisy" very low so no one else could hear it and each had a Baby Ruth. Then we were home, and he stepped back outside the circle and picked up the book. I don't think he came inside again. Maybe he did, but I don't remember it. (*SHE remains sitting, an ACTOR and ACTRESS move on from different entrances and confront each other. From time to time HE tries briefly to interrupt her.)*

ABORTION LAWYER

WOMAN. Suitable? No, actually that doesn't seem "suitable" to me. It is, and I'm sorry to say this, particularly coming from you, Brent, unacceptable after I've done all the bloody prep and legwork on this case, to tell me now, at this point, the Attorney General's office doesn't want *me* to prosecute it.

MAN. You know why—

WOMAN. And no, I don't think we get a "reverse spin" with a male attorney sticking it to abortion bombers and yes I do have an emotional view of the perpetrators and emphatically yes it makes me noticeably angry and they make me angry and you make me angry. Excuse me. Just hold on and I'll get this down to a rational level. Breathe in, breathe out. O.K.

Brent, you say my sex, no matter what I say, *is* an issue here. All right, granted for the sake of argument. Then it's good, it's an issue. Because without a female attorney it looks like the gender most affected either doesn't care or can't fight its own battles or isn't competent. They should know when they bomb medical facilities necessary to my freedom and well-being and then stand on a cross and wrap themselves in the flag that the cases will be fiercely prosecuted by the gender that has the most at stake. I am not only protected *by* legal process from these thugs, I *am* legal process and I will nail their self-righteous hides to the wall! (*Two other ACTRESSES enter and stand watching.*) Now I intend to do two things: I intend to prosecute this case and I intend to eat lunch. You can't do anything about number one and you are cordially invited to number two, my treat. How about it? (*SHE hits him fairly strongly on the shoulder for emphasis and exits.*)

SURPRISE

ONE of the two ACTRESSES who entered during the last speech sits on the hassock and speaks to the OTHER who leans over a chair.

What replaces surprise? There used to be surprises every day. The first time I asked a man to go to bed with me and he did. Finding out, suddenly, in college that I could do the work. Eating a brussel sprout and not minding. Realizing I actually had friends. Right through my thirties there were always surprises. Now I seem to see it all coming. Last week my brother-in-law stole change off my dresser. As soon as I knew it, I knew that I already knew he was capable of it. I suppose what happens is that you identify patterns. That in some larger sense you're always just playing percentage baseball. What surprises me is that I don't mind. What surprises me is that I have no nostalgia for surprises. What I guess interests me is why I'm getting such pleasure from a world I can second guess? We should be devastated, don't you think? I see pictures of Neptune, I see magnifications of aphids, I get mugged in a department store elevator but it's just more of what was already there. What I think is it's a theological/biological preparation for non-existence. I think I'm being prepared to leave. If the body releases chemicals that make pain more bearable then maybe it gives us a tolerance for repetition to make parting more bearable. That would be nice, don't you think? Otherwise we'd always want to stay. Maybe that's why we don't mind. Maybe that's why I'm not looking for any surprises. (*The SPEAKER moves the hassock back in front of the chair and exits. The ACTRESS listening moves up and sits in the armchair. A male ACTOR leans against the wall above her, bored and irritated as DUKE PHARSEE.*)

DUKE PHARSEE

Slapping herself and fanning herself simultaneously.

You in there, Duke Pharsee? You in there with the window open? I hope you know what you're doing in there? You are letting the mosquitoes roar in that open window come eat me alive like some road kill on the Hiawatha Bypass. You like a mosquito youself, Duke Pharsee. Eternally dressed in your yellow and black high school B-team letter jacket, suckin' up my money on food, on magazine subscriptions like some Asian tiger mosquito got into the country in a shipment of used tires down to Houston or Galveston or some humid place like that. You the same kind of immigrant to my country with the agenda of siphoning off my life blood through the agency of my unchecked sexual attraction. It is my opinion that the itch precedes the bite and even attracts it. Don't think I don't recognize you as the parasite you are because I do. Just because I prefer love to be a minor irritation and not a preoccupation leaves me precisely at the mercy of small-time hustlers like you. Now slam shut that window, throw down my *Cosmopolitan* magazine, get your little stinger in here an' let's see if we can pass the time before the good shows come on the T.V.

(*SHE throws a leg over the chair arm and puts her hands behind her head. Holds a beat. SHE then rises as the ACTRESS doing the next piece enters, and SHE and the MAN assist the woman delicately as SHE sits on the hassock.*)

NO PERSONALITY

They tested me twice on account of their dumbfoundedness the first time. And those results they came down the same way both times. Within a fraction of a point, so they told me. "How'd I do?" I'd say and they'd get this startled look and they'd say, "Well, Miss Latonia, we're pleased to say it's conclusive and definite, you don't have a personality." And I don't. I'd imagine there's a lot of us here and there. More than you think. It's hard to spot. You might be one. Now, if it turns out you are, don't feel bad. The head doctor he told me not to worry, it was kind of like being a punctuation mark. "There has to be a rest period between ideas and you're it. Look around you," he said, "there's a lot of people doing things and saying things, and things just go from bad to worse. They need you." Well, I'd never looked at it in that light, and I've tried not to get a swelled head over it. You may be stuck with a personality but that doesn't mean I can't respect you as a human being. (*SHE rises and moves downstage.*) The thing is that those that have a personality stew in it. They are sort of like telling the same joke to everybody. Whereas you and me are more freefloating, more restful to the passerby. More like watching water. The way things are, maybe we're the coming thing. (*SHE sits in the vinyl chair.*

Another ACTRESS enters and speaks to the empty rocker. This speech is one long build to a crescendo.)

NIGHTMARE DAUGHTER

This isn't fat, mother, this is bloom. The bloom on the rose. This is the radiance you read about in your two hundred romance novels a week. Don't look down on the carpet. I'm not on the carpet, mother. I'm here in the kitchen near the *refrigerator*. You caught me, sheriff! Two in the morning but you sniffed me out. I'm the Sara Lee bandido. The Che Guevara of Haagen-Dazs ice cream. By day my name is Nutra-Slim but come sunset, I rip the calorie counter from my heart, I trample grapefruit and carrot sticks and celery under my Nike Air Cross-Trainers and I expand. I fill with cholesterol like a deranged zeppelin. I inhale cheesecake, I eat the graham crackers box and all. Bits of packaged ham and pepperoni flake my disordered hair. My fangs drip butter almond swirl. And with my eyes rolled back in my head I crash through the wall into your pristine, chintz, unendurably perfect bedroom and I fling myself on you screaming, "This is me, mother. This is your nightmare daughter, you patronizing, priggish, punishing, unforgiving cancer of my life."

(SHE holds for two beats and sits in the chair she has been speaking to. Another ACTRESS

*moves on talking and sits in the armchair. SHE
never rises during this speech.)*

BEES

They ain't no honey climbers I know of anywhere outside Tennessee. Fadin' out. Back of the hills they long on that fresh, wild honey up on the cliffs for hard doctorin' an' love potions, but there ain't many will go up to get it. Ol' Grandpa did the high hangin' 'til his hands went stiff an' he couldn't hold rope. My brother, John Vale, took up, but he got his eyes stung out by a bee swarm covered his face like a black mask. Leaves me. See, how you do is seek out the swarms on the high cliff walls. A swarm will run fifteen feet across on a million bees. Got to drop down to 'em on a hemp twist ladder far as it takes. Sister Lilah, she hand climbs from below, sets a fire down of 'em, smokes that swarm off the comb. When they fly it's like the sun risin' 'cause there's that golden honeyhouse where it was black with bees. I come down the hemp twist ladder, carve slabs from the comb, let it fall to a willow wove basket, lower it down to the ground. Air around your head's got bees in it like ash from a fire. I'm to where I can take thirty, forty stings an' not hurt, nor swell, nor cry out. Only way they don't swarm ya's if you're right with Jesus an' cool as a stone. Johnny Vale he was doin' it on nerve 'cause he stole an' fornicated. Bee stung him on the nipple an' he took the name in vain. Lessen' fifteen seconds there was a thousand bees on his face exploded his eyes like a grape. Thousand bees together they's like a radio receiver for your heart. They know your sin's in your sweat. They can sense in your rhythm if you're ready for judgment. They know if there's guile or there's honey in the cells of your mind. See, Jesus is the order that holds off the Apocalypse. If he ain't in the bloodstream, life eats you alive.

(An ACTRESS already onstage lies erotically on the stage floor in front of the armchair. EVERYONE else exits.)

ONE MOMENT

God, you're beautiful. You must really work
out. I've been watching you ... from across the
street ... with binoculars. Wow, this is
embarrassing. I mean, not every minute. Not
every night. Only if there's nothing on television.
Then this afternoon ... boom ... there you are
with my doorman. Incredible. And now here we
are. Oh God that ... that feels ... euphoric. God, I
would never have thought of doing that with that.
Listen, before we make love would you mind
filling out this form? It's sort of a sexual history
and ... I don't know ... sort of ground rules. I'll
get you a copy of mine. The whole thing won't
take more than half an hour. Yes, yes touch me.
The phone's right there in case you have to call
people for details. God, I want you. The thing I
hate most is the man wearing a prophylactic for
oral sex. The first time I saw a man with a rubber
on his tongue I just about died laughing. Listen
this is hard to say but if your history seems dicey
I have a clear plastic shower curtain I could put
over you and we could just kind of hold each
other ... you know, after a milk bleach bath, or
we could just do visual sex or a phone date, I
mean if the surgical gloves put you off? Look, I
hate this, but would you mind if I checked your
gums? Here, you can look at mine. I know, let's

light the candles. (*The LIGHTS go down to a single pool of LIGHT on her*.) There. Intimacy.

STOLEN LIVES

Two MEN move on and sit on the arms of the armchair. Two WOMEN enter and stand back to back behind it. In this piece all lines in parentheses are spoken by Carl.

JAY. Me and my brother Carl (yo!) we took up with the DiMathis sisters in a time warp back in '78 ('79), '78, when we were sellin' cleanin' fluid door to door (see this spot on my tie?). They were two agoraphobics over two hundred pounds (dressed). Livin' their lives in every detail like Bette Davis. (It's true.) Invited us in on Friday, February 15, 1978 ...

(Whenever the women speak they do Bette Davis imitations.)

FLORENCE. Come on in, boys.
JAY. And when we walked out of there six weeks later it took seven damn years to get functional (or paroled). Florence DiMathis ...
FLORENCE. Don't stare at me, honey, unless you mean it.
JAY. ... preferred to live in the movie *Now Voyager* as a New England spinster who blossoms into a fashionable woman of poise and charm ...

FLORENCE. Let's not ask for the moon when we have the stars.

JAY. Whereas Alexis DiMathis (hoo-boy!) preferred *The Bride Came C.O.D.* (A temperamental oil heiress elopes with a Hollywood bandleader.)

ALEXIS. Hello, baby. You miss me?

JAY. There was two kinds of scenes they liked (scenes where we died) an' scenes where they died. In between we'd eat gourmet an' be chained to the bed for bouts of untamed sensuality (an' Shiatsu massage). It was a pretty good life. (Beat loadin' trucks for UPS.) The problem was *A Stolen Life* (1946 Warner Bros.) where Bette played identical twin sisters. Kate Bosworth (kindly and introspective) and the vivacious but thoroughly bitchy and unprincipled (Patricia). See, they both wanted to play Kate (cause she ended up with Glenn Ford). Me. (Well, you were older.) March 28, an' the DiMathis sisters was doin' their mornin' toilette (kinda wedged in) an' this pink water started runnin' out from under the bathroom door (oh-oh). "What's goin' on there, girls" (he yelled). An' the door slams open an' Alexis leans on the jamb in an off-the-shoulder black negligee (an' she says ...)

ALEXIS. Rafe darling. Patricia has been killed in a boating accident. I've been living her life. Can you ever forgive me? (Florence, she was in the tub face down.)

JAY. Shit. (Shit.) Hell we called the police in about one split second. (Freaked out.) Freaked out. (Shit.) They come squealin' up. Alexis starts yellin' ...

ALEXIS. My beautiful sister! Animals! Let them rot in hell!

JAY. (And when the cops hustle us out) She winks, see?

ALEXIS. Drifters! Murderers! Scum of the earth.

JAY. We served seven years in Tehatchapi (Maximum Security). Alexis, she would visit in a black veil and give us gloxinia.

ALEXIS. My heart is a hell, and you are my jailors.

JAY. (Don't ever get involved with Bette Davis, brothers.) She don't play straight parts.

SPIDERMAN

*All PERFORMERS from the last piece exit. Two
WOMEN enter. ONE sits on the armchair back
and ANOTHER on the seat. A third ACTRESS
enters and speaks.*

I seen things. Uh, huh! There's stuff goes on,
stuff! Sure there's crap too. Flying saucers, crap
like that. Every night there's fifteen, twenty
thousand husbands out doing what they
shouldn't, lose track of time, gets to be 3 in the
a.m. ... You think a couple of them don't go
home tell their wives they was kidnapped by little
orange men in a glowing cigar-shaped object?
Uh, huh. On the contrary you got the bonafide
unexplainable. Me. A common person. Butter my
toast like the pope, right? Right. Listen, I'm on
my honeymoon. Indianapolis, the Holiday Inn,
honeymoon suite. He wants mirrors on the ceiling
... like I want an aerial view. Sixteenth floor.
Fire! Fire! Open the door, we got your proverbial
wall of flame. Great. The last thing I'll remember
will be the missionary position in a mirror. We go
out on the balcony. This big. Inferno time. Can
we jump? No. Can we go back in? No. I turn to
my husband, I say, "Hey, at least we came before
we went." Tears run down his cheeks. I look
down, a guy is climbing the side of the building.

No ropes. What is he wearing? You got it. Blue and red. It's Spiderman. I'm not pulling your chain, man. I got saved on my honeymoon in the famous Indianapolis Holiday Inn fire by a super hero. Uh, huh. You think I'm kidding, right? He has me on his shoulders and my husband by the belt, we go straight down the outside glass. I say, "Hey, Spidey, where's your pal Superman?" He says, "Superman has no dick. He's in therapy." Stuff. I seen stuff. You want to know something else? My marriage broke up, I date him. You want to know something else? I'm pregnant. Weird hormonal chemistry, you know? Sometimes filament spins out of my body. I'm beginning to climb. (*Her eyes fill with tears.*) I'm beginning to climb. (*SHE sits.*)

ROLLER COASTER

*The ACTRESS speaking and the ACTRESS
above her on the chair back sometimes move in
unison to create the roller coaster.*

The gargoyle. It had four 360-degree loop-de-
loops and a first fall that could put your heart in
your forehead! What a beauty! It had incline roll
drops, one left, one right that felt like they went
on to Chicago and a slow draw up at 90 degrees
that stood the hair on your toes on end! Me and
Sis waited two damn hours to get on that machine
an' when we jumped on, it took off. There was a
gent there, I yelled, "Hey, man, the roll bars," an'
he looked startled but we were on the incline and I
yelled down, "She's not in, Goddamnit. Throw
the switch. Shut it down!" I could see somebody
start to run but we crested the top an' it took off.
"Grab the rail. Left hand. Now me. Not there, the
belt. The belt! Let me get an arm behind ... up ...
move forward ... behind you. I got it. I got you.
Hold on. Hold fucking on. Oh my God. Oh my
Jesus. Stop this son of a bitch!" We hit the loops.
One, two, I saw Sis bite through her lip. Three,
four, and her hand on the rail moved to her face
and swinging out of the fourth loop she went out
of the car in this rising arc making a shy little
high-pitched noise and I wrench around and she

was lying out sideways in the air and she saw me and she waved. Like you were supposed to wave when you left people. Like she lived in the air and she'd never come down. Like it was the wildest best part of the ride. Like she was still alive.

(The SPEAKER exits leaving the ACTRESS who began the evening sitting as she first did on the armchair back in a special.)

ENDINGS

I sat in the chair by the bed watching him sleep until I ached from sitting and then went out to the tool shed where I had hidden the suitcase and put it by the door of the car and stood without knowing what to do next in the yard listening to the trucks go by on the freeway down below. He was so good about beginnings and endings and summing things up and knowing what must be done and explaining why it was the way it was now and I'd never seemed to have a talent for it. I owed him a good solid ending that he could carry around with him and trot out on occasions and gatherings but for the life of me I couldn't think of one and it was a serious, hopeless failing and couldn't be forgiven. I thought of so many things that had happened and then more things and more things, but I couldn't make an explanation of them so I went back in and lay down beside him because if you can't explain endings, then you probably don't deserve one. And he shifted and touched me lightly and that was familiar, and the shadows in the room were familiar, and the beginnings of the birds were familiar. And as I fell asleep I thought, well, that's all right, it's going on then. It's going on. (*The LIGHTS dim slowly.*)

Curtain Call

APPENDIX

The author includes the following pieces for possible substitutions if casting or context would be improved by them.

HAMS

Before they put the highway through, well, I looked out over actual living grass. There was a cypress row and past that, scrub woods, wild flowers. I bought the house because of what was across the street. Nothing. Nothing was across the street. Dusk time I'd sit on my porch ... listen, never mind. Now I have trucks, more trucks. All right, life changes. Then they put up the billboard. I've got six windows in front. Out each window I see a cartoon Shakespeare three stories high with a lampshade on his head carving a ham the size of my Volkswagen, and in day-glo letters it reads, "Ham It Up." Daybreak, noontime, late night ... "Ham It Up." I buy a chainsaw. I buy Army fatigues. August 12, one a.m., I cut that mother down. Ecowarrior! August 17th, it's back, it's bigger, it has stadium lights. Three canned hams tap-dancing in top hats with canes and three stories high on countersunk steel pillars it says "Pearls Among Swine." I sleep no more. I buy climbing gear. Attach chains to the top. Rent a 16-wheeler. Pop that clutch and I topple that son-of-a-bitch like Ozymandias! And I dance, and dance, and drink myself insensate, and sleep eighteen hours. When I regain consciousness, they're putting up the new sign. It's a sliced ham with wings and a halo, playing a harp. "Pig Heaven."

There is a moment in life when you know what you will become. When you fully understand that there is only process, only struggle and that heroism is not the single reflexive blow, it is the power of repetition without hope. And when you know that, you must not hesitate, you must not vacillate, you must not ruminate, you sell out! After that, believe me, the world moves on and the prices go down.

PASSING THE TIME

Are you ... you're going to think I'm crazy ... Are you passing the time? Sometimes I think ... never mind. A voice tells me that I'm "passing the time." A key meeting, for instance, the presentation to the client, wild adrenalin, jobs on the line, it sells. People are ecstatic, they're like hugging and ... look it's a triumph and ... well, I hear this cool laconic humorous voice saying "Well, that's passing the time."

I've had it happen when I'm making love. I've heard it when I take flowers out to mother's cemetery. I bought a new car. Hey, that's a big thing, that's a twelve thousand dollar thing. I'm driving it off the lot, and I hear this whisper in my ear, "Say, this is passing the time." Things I love to do, people I want to be with, moments I've been waiting for, "Well, that's passing the time."

As if the real thing, the real, real thing, the thing that isn't "passing the time" is always where I'm not. And I can't seem to make the simple, clear gesture, say the authentic thing, just for God's sake be here. Just *be* here. I'm living just ... just a little *off*, you know just infinitesimally wrong. Missing my life by inches. Passing the time.

HEALIN'

Healin' don't ordinarily git born on you as is much supposed. More than usual it's just passed along. Aunt Jesse Colt she give it to me. Told me I was an ugly child, so I needed talents. Said, "Here, girl," an' she cupped a hand over each of my eyes and blew that gift in between the fingers. My healin' gifts is three. I can heal burns, cure the babies' yella thrash, an' draw out the dog day blues.Women gits them blues in the heart of the heat. Just lie about, good for nothin', cryin' over who knows what, bein' miserable an' pissin' all over their men. Man gets somethin' of the kind, but you can't heal on it, he got to drink it out. Now I'll sit down by a woman, read her Ezekiel, chapter seventeen, verse six. Parch me some red pepper at the fire. Powder it, cook it in a tea, add bayberry, two tablespoons white corn liquor, and sing what I please. She don't see a man for three days she'll cure. You don't want such blues there's three avoidances. Don't get married 'til forty, don't travel more'n fifty miles from where you're born, and don't lie with no red-headed man plays the banjo in a public place. Them three I know from personal experience. They're just incurable. Any other way you get 'em, you send for me. I got travelin' gifts.

SOUNDS YOU MAKE

There's a very particular sound I associate with you. Just the smallest exhalation of breath. So light sometimes it's just on the edge of being heard. But you mean me to hear it. It's not spontaneous or surprised. It's meant to wound. It's meant to delicately remind me of my unreason. It intimates something soiled and hopelessly emotional. That you by all rights should disdain or reject in me but at the same time it makes you unassailably good because all you do is make the sound and that resigned, fluttering palms up gesture and stay reasonably silent in the face of what, if you did speak, you might call my *provocations.* And every time you do it, I feel vaguely ashamed because *I* haven't been good, *I* haven't been accepting or forgiving or forebearing. I've had the immense bad taste to feel something when you didn't instigate it, or ask for it or, worse yet, simply weren't in the mood for it. And the worst of it is that it's so painfully clear how much you enjoy what you're feeling about me and how you want me to hear you feeling it. So that I realize that now what used to be my pleasure in your company has become this longing to never, never, never hear you make that sound again. Never. Never.

SOFTBALL

A game of fast-pitch softball. A PITCHER. SHE throws one.

God, I hate softball. Two more outs I got my three hundred sixty-third no-hitter. (*SHE pitches.*)

Two more games we got our eighteenth straight world championship. Kind of takes the thrill out it. (*SHE pitches.*)

Another damn strikeout. Last July I fell asleep in the middle of an inning on a three-two count. (*SHE pitches.*)

I'm a damn immortal for $600 a week playing for a solid pack tuna company I wouldn't feed to my cat. (*SHE pitches.*)

I had this record in the Bigs I would own a state. Bonuses! Don't talk to me about bonuses. Every time I strike out twenty, I get a free cheese pizza. Toppings is extra. (*SHE pitches.*)

God I hate this batter. Guy doing the stats says 80% of my career strikeouts is blondes with natural curl. (*SHE pitches.*)

Ball? My ass that was a ball, ump. You're calling a strike zone about as big as her tits. I take that back. Her tits was the strike zone, we'd a had a twenty-seven straight walks here. (*SHE pitches.*)

We win. Whoopee. Time for the old shower,
if there was a shower. Sometimes I bring water to
the park in a ziplock bag. Go back to my motel,
switch on the light bulb, see half those blondes I
struck out on the pornography channel ... have
me some cold nachos and a warm Seven-up. Self
satisfaction! That's what I got. I got a world of
self satisfaction. Women's sports.

Also By

Jane Martin

ANTON IN SHOW BUSINESS

THE BOY WHO ATE THE MOON

CEMENTVILLE

CRIMINAL HEARTS

CUL-DE-SAC

FLAMING GUNS OF THE PURPLE SAGE

GOOD BOYS

KEELY AND DU

MAKING THE CALL

MIDDLE-AGED WHITE GUYS

MR. BUNDY

POMP AND CIRCUMSTANCE

SHASTA RUE

SUMMER

TALKING WITH

TATTOO

TRAVELIN' SHOW

WHAT MAMA DON'T KNOW

SKIN DEEP
Jon Lonoff

Comedy / 2m, 2f / Interior Unit Set

In *Skin Deep*, a large, lovable, lonely-heart, named Maureen Mulligan, gives romance one last shot on a blind-date with sweet awkward Joseph Spinelli; she's learned to pepper her speech with jokes to hide insecurities about her weight and appearance, while he's almost dangerously forthright, saying everything that comes to his mind. They both know they're perfect for each other, and in time they come to admit it.

They were set up on the date by Maureen's sister Sheila and her husband Squire, who are having problems of their own: Sheila undergoes a non-stop series of cosmetic surgeries to hang onto the attractive and much-desired Squire, who may or may not have long ago held designs on Maureen, who introduced him to Sheila. With Maureen particularly vulnerable to both hurting and being hurt, the time is ripe for all these unspoken issues to bubble to the surface.

"Warm-hearted comedy … the laughter was literally show-stopping. A winning play, with enough good-humored laughs and sentiment to keep you smiling from beginning to end."
- TalkinBroadway.com

"It's a little Paddy Chayefsky, a lot Neil Simon and a quick-witted, intelligent voyage into the not-so-tranquil seas of middle-aged love and dating. The dialogue is crackling and hilarious; the plot simple but well-turned; the characters endearing and quirky; and lurking beneath the merriment is so much heartache that you'll stand up and cheer when the unlikely couple makes it to the inevitable final clinch."
- NYTheatreWorld.Com

THE OFFICE PLAYS
Two full length plays by Adam Bock

THE RECEPTIONIST
Comedy / 2m, 2f / Interior

At the start of a typical day in the Northeast Office, Beverly deals effortlessly with ringing phones and her colleague's romantic troubles. But the appearance of a charming rep from the Central Office disrupts the friendly routine. And as the true nature of the company's business becomes apparent, The Receptionist raises disquieting, provocative questions about the consequences of complicity with evil.

"...Mr. Bock's poisoned Post-it note of a play."
- New York Times

"Bock's intense initial focus on the routine goes to the heart of *The Receptionist's* pointed, painfully timely allegory... elliptical, provocative play..."
- Time Out New York

THE THUGS
Comedy / 2m, 6f / Interior

The Obie Award winning dark comedy about work, thunder and the mysterious things that are happening on the 9th floor of a big law firm. When a group of temps try to discover the secrets that lurk in the hidden crevices of their workplace, they realize they would rather believe in gossip and rumors than face dangerous realities.

"Bock starts you off giggling, but leaves you with a chill."
- Time Out New York

"... a delightfully paranoid little nightmare that is both more chillingly realistic and pointedly absurd than anything John Grisham ever dreamed up."
- New York Times

SAMUELFRENCH.COM

NO SEX PLEASE, WE'RE BRITISH
Anthony Marriott and Alistair Foot

Farce / 7 m, 3 f / Interior

A young bride who lives above a bank with her husband who is the assistant manager, innocently sends a mail order off for some Scandinavian glassware. What comes is Scandinavian pornography. The plot revolves around what is to be done with the veritable floods of pornography, photographs, books, films and eventually girls that threaten to engulf this happy couple. The matter is considerably complicated by the man's mother, his boss, a visiting bank inspector, a police superintendent and a muddled friend who does everything wrong in his reluctant efforts to set everything right, all of which works up to a hilarious ending of closed or slamming doors. This farce ran in London over eight years and also delighted Broadway audiences.

"Titillating and topical."
- "NBC TV"

"A really funny Broadway show."
- "ABC TV"

BLUE YONDER
Kate Aspengren

Dramatic Comedy / Monolgues and scenes
12f (can be performed with as few as 4 with doubling) / Unit Set

A familiar adage states, "Men may work from sun to sun, but women's work is never done." In Blue Yonder, the audience meets twelve mesmerizing and eccentric women including a flight instructor, a firefighter, a stuntwoman, a woman who donates body parts, an employment counselor, a professional softball player, a surgical nurse professional baseball player, and a daredevil who plays with dynamite among others. Through the monologues, each woman examines her life's work and explores the career that she has found. Or that has found her.